To all the dreamers, thinkers, makers, and creators
making your way—let your light shine!—O.R.-P.

To all the makers,
never stop making your own way.—A.P.

Grateful acknowledgments to the following people at the National Museum
of African American History and Culture for their assistance and expertise:
Reneé S. Anderson, PhD, Head of Collections; Kinshasha Holman Conwill, Deputy Director;
Candra Flanagan, Director of Teaching and Learning; Paul Gardullo, PhD, Supervisory
Curator History; Anna Hindley, Director of Early Childhood Education; Danielle Lancaster,
Management Support Specialist; Michele Gates Moresi, PhD, Supervisory Museum Curator
of Collections; Fleur Paysour, Public Affairs Specialist; Doug Remley, Rights and
Reproduction Specialist; Esther J. Washington, Director of Education

Special thanks to the following people at Smithsonian Enterprises:
Kealy Gordon, Product Development Manager; Jill Corcoran, Director, Licensed Publishing;
Brigid Ferraro, Vice President, Business Development and Licensing;
Carol LeBlanc, President

Additional appreciation to Donna Limerick
for all of her insight and passion

Mae Makes a Way

THE TRUE STORY OF MAE REEVES, HAT & HISTORY MAKER

BY OLUGBEMISOLA Rhuday-Perkovich

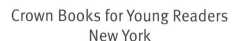
ILLUSTRATIONS BY ANDREA PIPPINS

Smithsonian

NATIONAL MUSEUM of AFRICAN AMERICAN HISTORY & CULTURE

Crown Books for Young Readers
New York

Ruffly skirts and puffy sleeves! Fussy frills and rows of ribbons! Grandma Lula dressed little Mae all fancy, like a tiny doll.

Mae didn't want to be a doll. She wanted to go outside and play in the dirt! But in those fancy clothes, Mae told a beautiful story. She offered hope during hard days.

By the early 1900s, when Mae was a girl, slavery had officially ended in the United States. But new segregation laws kept Black people apart and unequal. Instead of liberty and justice, Black citizens like Mae and her family faced violence and oppression. Little Mae in her ruffles and ribbons brought joy in the midst of much suffering.

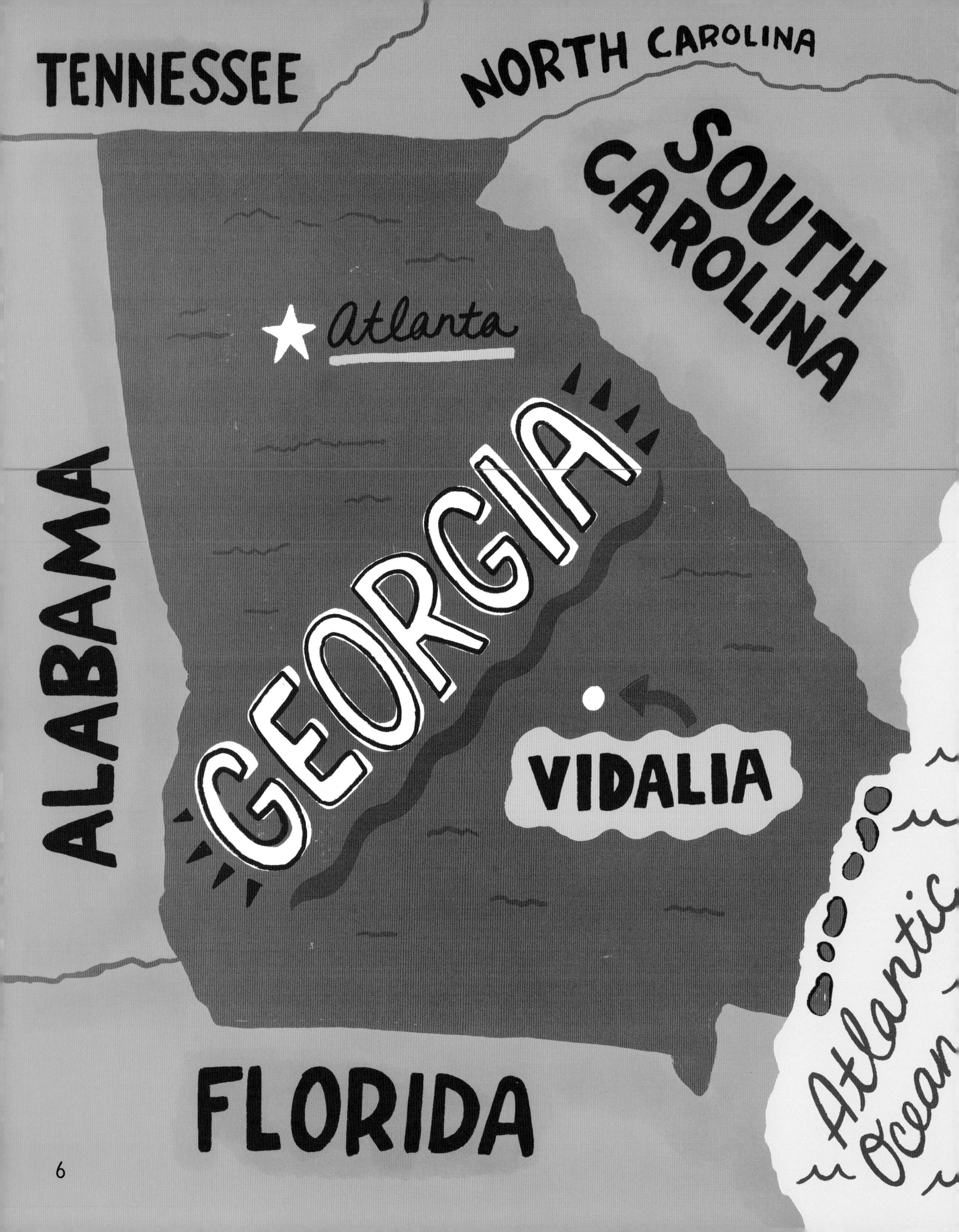

TENNESSEE

NORTH CAROLINA

SOUTH CAROLINA

★ *Atlanta*

GEORGIA

ALABAMA

VIDALIA

FLORIDA

Atlantic Ocean

Mae's small hometown was in the segregated South. Vidalia, Georgia, did not have many opportunities for Black families to live their best lives and do what they dreamed. But as Mae grew, she made her own ways to have fun. At school, Mae wrote plays—and she was also the director *and* star. She designed and sewed fancy clothes for her dolls. Mae made joys, but sorrow came. Mae's parents died when she was only fourteen, and she and her younger siblings went to live with her grandmother.

In the 1920s, lingering turmoil from World War I brought destruction to the world stage and the Jazz Age was not jumping for everyone. Black families faced more hardship and pain, and children like Mae had to work like grown-ups. One brother shined shoes. Another worked as a babysitter for a white family. Mae was in charge of her younger sisters and brothers, so she learned how to take good care of other people.

Like many young Black women of the South in the 1920s and 1930s, Mae became a teacher. She worked in a one-room schoolhouse with a potbellied stove. She was only a teenager; some of her students were very young, and others were much older—even older than Mae! But she taught them all.

Mae was also a newspaper writer, entertaining readers with stories of fancy and fun parties and events in the community. She found ways to celebrate the beauty of her neighbors' spirits, even when there was ugliness and hurt in their lives.

THE GREAT MIGRATION

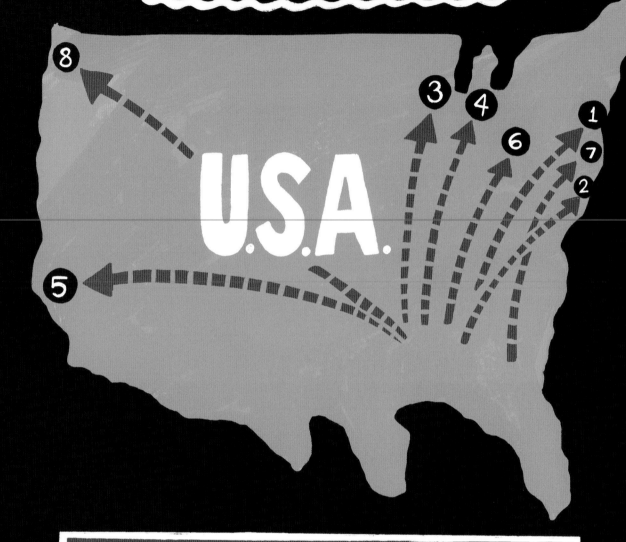

CITIES AFRICAN AMERICANS MIGRATED TO
1 New York   3 Chicago   5 Los Angeles   7 Newark
2 Philadelphia   4 Detroit   6 Pittsburgh   8 Seattle

During those days, thousands of Black people fled the persecution and cruelty of their segregated southern hometowns for integrated northern cities. Mae was one of those who resisted the voices of oppression that said there was no way out. Mae decided to make a way.

With ideas in her head and those doll-sewing skills in her hands, she traveled by train from Georgia all the way up north to Chicago, Illinois.

At the Chicago School of Millinery, people made many kinds of head coverings, and lots of people needed them—in those days, hats on heads were as common as shoes on feet.

But even in integrated cities, Black people lived unequal lives. Black women were often treated as though they were invisible. When a Black woman went out wearing a hat and gloves, there was a chance she'd be shown more respect. Hats were a way for these queens to be SEEN, shining a light on the dignity they always had.

Mae used wire, fabric, steam, and most of all her imagination to create crowns. She made sassy hats, classy hats, high headpieces, and low caps. She used bows and baubles, created ruffles and bustle. Each hat was an original, like Mae herself.

At the Chicago School of Millinery, Black students and white students learned and worked together, side by side. When Mae went back down south to her segregated town and segregated school, she remembered the northern ways. She dreamed of one day making a wide-open way for side by side in her life, all year-round, every day.

Mae kept on learning up north and teaching down south.

She got married and had a child, William, called Sonny. But when her husband died in an accident, Mae had to figure out how to take care of her son alone.

One of her older brothers lived up north, in Philadelphia. Mae visited and saw Black people from small southern towns living big northern dreams. She decided to pack her high hopes and make a new way with her son in this City of Brotherly Love.

There, Mae worked in a shop, helping ladies buy glamorous get-ups: dresses, purses, shoes, and jewelry. "I like to make them pretty," she said. Mae also learned how to run a business—buying supplies and refilling stock, managing people, and decorating the store windows.

When the shoppers found out about Mae's head-topping masterpieces, they all wanted a bit of her magic. So she started making hats to sell: fun hats with feathers, fancy hats with flowers, and everything in between. A lady could bring in an old hat with a brim and Mae would transform it into a new twisty turban. "I felt like an artist," said Mae.

Tulle

SCISSORS

SILK FLOWERS

thread

Feathers

Velvet! Brocade! Satins and silks! She made hats for a trip to the grocery store or a fancy party, for any occasion or time of day. "Mae of Philadelphia" was famous! More and more ladies came from all over for one of Mae's original crowns, and her business grew and grew.

Mae still wanted to make her own way.

A Black-owned business was the kind of progress that most whites didn't want. Many establishments would not even serve Black people. But Black communities "made a way out of no way" by building their own businesses and schools. Philadelphia was a center of Black business, including banks that were important to dreamers like Mae.

In 1941, when she was only twenty-eight years old, Mae went to one of those Black banks, Citizens and Southern Bank, and she got a $500 loan. And then she marched right down the street and rented a space on the first floor of a building on busy South Street.

Many Black people had settled in that area, and it was full of restaurants, clubs, and other garment businesses. Now Mae owned one too. With that loan, she became the first Black woman to own a business on South Street, and she hung a photo of the bank president, "Major" Wright, in her shop for many years. Mae's Millinery was in the front of the building, and she and her little boy, Sonny, made their home in the back. Mae was making a living, and she was making a life as "Mae of Philadelphia."

Mae made everyone feel their best selves with her glimmery hats, shimmery hats, snappy hats, and happy hats. "I just made sure I had the stuff women wanted, no matter what skin color they were!" she said. When famous Black entertainers like Marian Anderson, Lena Horne, and Ella Fitzgerald came to town, they left with one of Mae's crowns. Rich white ladies shopped at Mae's too, along with housekeepers, teachers, and the faithful church ladies who believed that Sunday mornings were for showstoppers. Whether a lady click-clacked in high heels from a shiny black limousine or stepped, slow and tired, from the public bus, Mae made magic for each and every one.

Lena Horne

Marian Anderson

Ella Fitzgerald

If a customer didn't have the money to pay right then and there, Mae would trust them to take the hat and pay another day. "Guess what," said Mae. "They always did!"

23

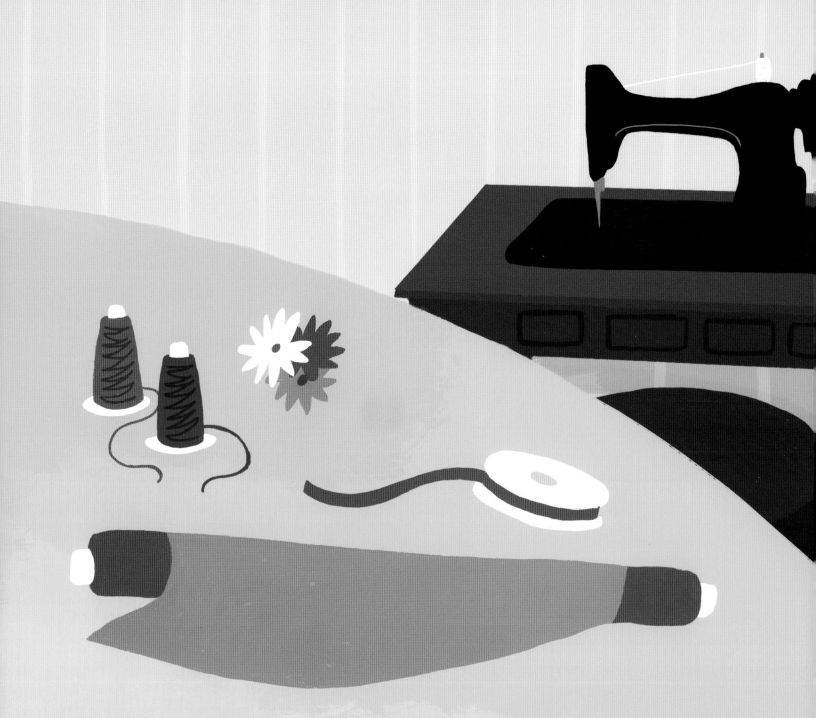

As Mae's little boy grew, she saw that he needed something more than the South Street hustle-bustle. She bought a home in West Philadelphia and ran her business from her dining room. Where Mae went, her customers followed. Sometimes Mae the mom would be cooking dinner in the kitchen and helping with homework, and Mae the milliner would run to the dining room to help a customer. "You do what you got to do. I had to work with my family, and make a living too," she said. Many department stores in that area did not serve or hire Black people, so along with her handmade creations, Mae's business also offered important job opportunities and space to *be*. If a customer was lucky, they could stay for one of Mae's home-cooked meals. Mae always made more than enough.

Mae fell in love and married again. She had two more children, Donna and Reginald. She kept making a living and making a life. She loved baseball and cheered on the Black teams when they came to town. She and her husband Joel stepped out to fancy dances, and sometimes they'd even hop a train out of town for a good party.

Mae volunteered with local and national groups, from her church to the
NAACP civil rights organization. Mae "lifted as she climbed," raising money to
help others in her community and driving older ladies around town in her shiny
car, wherever they wanted to go. Every summer, she'd close the shop and take
the whole family to enjoy weeks of sun and sea air at the New Jersey shore. She'd
drive neighborhood kids to the beach so that they could enjoy the sun and sea air
too. People called her "Mom" or "Momma Mae" because she made a way for
many to feel like family.

As Mae's family grew and changed, so did her business and community. It was time to do new things to build better tomorrows, even though many people wanted Black women to stay stuck in yesterdays. Could Mae make a new way?

The streets of West Philadelphia buzzed with the energy from the nearby "El" train and all kinds of businesses: Woolworth's drugstore! Shoe stores! Banks! Dress shops! and more. But all those businesses were owned by white people.

Then in 1947, a new neon sign gleamed from a shop window with welcome and promise: "Mae's Millinery" at 41 N. 60th Street. And where Mae went, her loyal customers followed—plus new ones from north to south and east to west.

As Mae's business grew, she brought other family members from the South to join her up north. She gave them jobs in her shop and made a way for many more. Mae's brother Jack began working in the store as a salesman. He was charming and stylish, like Mae—so Mr. Jack sold a lot of hats, as fast as Mae could create them.

Mae guaranteed that each lady had her own hat story to tell. "You can't just plop a hat on your head," Mae would say. "You have to work with it." She'd invite them to sit in front of the mirror to try on her creations. She'd bend and fold, and sometimes she'd offer them a pair of gloves and a handbag too. If a lady was a little down and droopy, Mae would spritz some perfume into the air or give her a touch of lipstick to bring out her bloom. She'd pour a cup of hot, fragrant tea and lend a listening ear.

Mae taught her children the lessons she'd learned. When her daughter, Donna, was born, Mae put her oldest child, Sonny, in charge of his baby sister. He'd push little Donna in her stroller right down to his stickball games, where he could play *and* keep watch. Later, little brother Reginald enjoyed fishing with their dad, and Donna worked in the shop with Mae. Sometimes Mae had Donna dress up in a black dress and pearls—with a hat, of course, because, as Mae would say, "You're not fully dressed unless you wear a hat."

William,
Wish
you were
here!
xo ♡
Mae

William R.
South Street
Philadelphia, PA
U.S.A.

PARIS

Mae and Donna would zip across state lines to New York City or over the ocean to Paris on exciting adventures to find the latest and best feathers, ribbons, and trimmings for Mae's elegant crowns. During the busiest times, like Easter and Mother's Day, family and friends filled the shop, helping Mae make the eye-catching special-occasion showstoppers that made her famous. Mae's best friends even became "Mae's girls," modeling her creations at fashion shows and fancy teas.

Mae was Black, a woman, a mother, and a business owner. None of those were easy to be in the 1940s and 1950s. As Black leaders organized for justice and neighbors shared resources, Mae also made ways for others in her community to prosper. Mae and her husband Joel were involved in local politics, and on Election Day, they would roll the giant polling machines into Mae's Millinery so that their Black neighbors were able to vote. People came in and enjoyed cookies, tea, and conversation about how to build the community and dream for the next generation.

As times changed, ladies' relationships with hats did too. In the 1960s and 1970s, fluffy Afros and poofy bouffants meant that Mae's elegant creations and spectacular crowns were no longer in high demand.

But one faithful group still wanted elegant hats and dignified hats, flowery hats and feathery hats. Church ladies needed their Sunday-morning showstoppers. So she kept her shop open for those special clients for many years.

In 1997, when she was eighty-five years old, Mae's smile still shone. "I'm very happy because I believe doing good things in life makes you happy. I can say that I've worked hard to make others happy too."

As Mae got older, it got harder and harder for her to climb up and down the steps from her home to the store. For more than fifty years, she had made many people happy with her hats, but it was time to move on. She went to live in a special place with other elders, sharing memories of her millinery magic. Many of the young workers in Mae's new home had visited her shop with their mothers and family members. They had Mae's Millinery tales too!

Hats on South

In 2009, a new national museum was announced. The National Museum of African American History and Culture would be the first of its kind, sharing the many stories and memories of Black people in the United States. The museum curators asked African Americans across the country to bring their special family items and stories to them, so that they could build a museum collection for all the world to see.

Mae's shop sat, just as she had left it, with her life's work still inside—hats, molds, ribbons, and the neon sign, frozen in time. Donna, now a documentary producer, wondered if an important museum would care about the story of Mae's still-stunning creations.

When the museum people came to her shop, they cared about Mae's work—a lot. Mae's creations were more than hats—they were history.

ITEM #100123561
MAE REEVES

Mae Reeves made a loving, creative life with her family, including her children, grandchildren, great-grandchildren— and even great-great-grandchildren!

She died when she was 104 years old.

Her magnificent work and unquenchable spirit live on.

She made the crowns, and we can hold them in our hearts.

Mae, like so many, made a way out of no way,

so we can hold our heads high

and our dreams even higher.

An Interview with Mae Reeves's Daughter, Donna Limerick

What was Mae's family life like?

My mom and dad had a wonderful and loving relationship. They were a team and known as a "power couple" in the community. My dad, Joel, had a part-time catering business, while Mae ran her hat business. They often had lovely cocktail and dinner parties for family and friends. Besides good food and drinks, their guests could dance all evening, thanks to local musicians who came by. Mae enjoyed playing the piano. My brother Reggie and I would sit at the top of the stairs watching it all, until Mom or Dad noticed. They would bring a treat and wave us to bed.

Did Mae have any other hobbies?

Mae loved sports. Her father, Samuel Grant, was a baseball umpire in Vidalia. He taught her all about baseball. When Mae and her first child, Sonny, moved to Philly, she took him to all the Black League baseball games. Like most African Americans at that time, they got dressed up in stylish outfits and hats . . . to cheer on the players.

She also enjoyed cooking big meals for family and friends. Her special desserts were blackberry or peach cobblers. She would easily cook three or four at one time for us to eat.

Did Mae have any nicknames?

My mother did not have any nicknames . . . but I acquired a few because of her. For example, some family members called me Donna Mae as a child and still do today. Mae's customers referred to me as "Mae's Daughter," when I began working in her hat shop. I often wondered, Why can't they remember my real name? ☺

What were some of the things you did as a Mae's Millinery employee?

At age sixteen, I began working in Mae's Millinery on Saturdays and holidays, including Easter and Mother's Day. I worked as a salesperson, showing hats to customers, doing minor things like sewing, steaming hats, or rearranging them in the store window or glass cabinets. I also helped decorate the shop window each season. We would buy special paper or fabric, artificial flowers, and other items to enhance the hats. I had to wear pearls and a black dress while working in the store. My girlfriends would stop by the hat shop wearing jeans and T-shirts and asked my mom if they could work in her shop if they wore clothes like me. She always said, "Sure, honey, a black dress and pearls are all you'll need to work here."

How were you involved in the exhibit?

The Smithsonian staff "hit the nail on the head," as Mae would say. They re-created her lovely shop with fifty years of her personal items, including hats, jewelry, and furniture, like the white antique table where women from all walks of life, both white and Black, socialites, professionals, and working women, sat side by side trying on Mae's amazing hats. The antique French red love seat is one of Mae's special items I always wanted to keep! But when the museum came calling, I knew the museum's exhibit was a much better place than my home.

What's one memorable experience with Mae that you remember?

Just before the museum opened in 2016, Oprah's magazine featured Oprah's Favorite Things at the museum. The museum's founding director, Lonnie Bunch, and his curators chose five of the most storied artifacts to showcase from over 37,000 items they acquired. One of the items was a beautiful baby blue cloche straw hat with a very long, soft tulle veil that draped around the neckline. When I took a copy of the article to show Mom she was totally astonished, and we both shed a few tears of joy. She could not believe that one of her hat creations was featured in the same article as Harriet Tubman's hymnal and Chuck Berry's big red Cadillac. I will never forget the sweet smile on her face and glow in her eyes.

An Interview with Dr. Reneé S. Anderson, Head of Collections at the NMAAHC

What was unusual or particularly striking about Mae Reeves's work?
What was striking about Mae was her ability to anticipate the fashion desires and needs of her customers. She created hats to fit every event from day wear to sportswear, special occasions to church wear, and even mourning veils. It was also apparent that Mae could use standard materials of excellent quality to create "showstopping" fashions. Her creativity indicated she was a Master Milliner.

How did you choose which of her hats to display?
Our teams selected hats based on our desire to build a collection that spanned the time frame that Mae's Millinery was open.

How did you go about re-creating Mae's Millinery in the Smithsonian exhibit? What elements of Mae's work did you want to share?
We wanted the exhibit to feel like a creative nook filled with Mae's equipment and supplies to showcase her development and execution of designs. We considered which furniture to include for the exhibit and created size templates based around them. Through a discussion with the curator, we determined how long each object could safely be displayed, and detailed notes were written for the selected objects as well as photographs of the layout. These notes and images were then shared with the exhibition design team and formal drawings were created for use during the installation process to bring Mae's shop to life in its new space.

Will the exhibit change over time?
Yes, the exhibit has and will continue to change. Fragile objects on display are rotated to help preserve this collection for the future as well as to make them available for research.

At the National Museum of African American History and Culture (NMAAHC), **Dr. Reneé S. Anderson** coordinates and oversees program activities related to collections management and exhibition preparation. She served as the Principal Investigator for The Andrew W. Mellon Foundation NMAAHC Collections Grant, which supported the opening of the museum in 2016 and its ongoing exhibitions and efforts.

About the NMAAHC

The National Museum of African American History and Culture opened in September 2016 as the nineteenth museum of the Smithsonian, the largest museum complex and research organization in the world. To date, the museum has welcomed more than seven million visitors and is proud to be the nation's largest and most comprehensive cultural destination devoted exclusively to exploring, documenting, and showcasing the African American story and its impact on American and world history.

Mae's Millinery closed its doors in 1997, but Mae instructed her family not to touch the shop. In 2010, curators connected with Mae's daughter, Donna Limerick. Awed by Mae's story and her groundbreaking designs, the Smithsonian has re-created portions of Mae's Millinery, including its original red-neon sign, sewing machine, and of course, beautiful hats, as a permanent installment in the *Power of Place* exhibition. You can visit the museum in Washington, DC, and online at nmaahc.si.edu.

Photo Credits

Sources

Blackwell, Laura. "Momma Mae, The 'Hat Lady' Turns 100." *Westside Weekly*, November 8–12, 2012.

"Citizens and Southern Bank Historical Marker: Behind the Marker." Explore PA History. explorepahistory.com/hmarker.php?markerId=1-A-32D.

Fisher, Elizabeth. "Hats off to God." *Catholic Philly*, October 7, 2010. catholicphilly.com/2010/10/news/hats-off-to-god/.

Frazier, Lisa. "Church Ladies and Their Big, Bold Hats: A Fading Tradition." *The Washington Post*. Masslive.com, April 14, 2012. Updated March 24, 2019. masslive.com /living/2012/04/church_ladies_and_their_big_bold_hats_a_fading_tradition.html.

Goin' North. "Citizens' and Southern: The People's Bank." goinnorth.org/exhibits/show/charles-ealy/citizens-and-southern.

Jones, Rebecca. "Hats off to Mom!" *African American News*.

Limerick, Donna, in discussion with the author, August 6, 2018 and September 6, 2018.

"Mae Reeves: Custom-Made Hats Extraordinaire." Black Then, October 9, 2018. blackthen.com/mae-reeves-custom-made-hats-extraordinaire/.

"Monday Open Thread: Showstoppers! African American Milliners." Pragmatic Obots Unite, December 9, 2013. pragmaticobotsunite2018.com/monday-open-thread -showstoppers-african-american-milliners/.

NMAAHC. "Mae's Millinery Shop." *American History Through an African American Lens*, April 9, 2017. nmaahc.tumblr.com/post/159390897172/maes-millinery-shop.

Page, Lisa Frazier. "Church Ladies and Hats: A Thing of the Past?" *The Washington Post*, April 7, 2012. washingtonpost.com/local /church-ladies-and-hats-a-thing-of -the-past/2012/04/07/gIQAgH7v1S_story.html?noredirect=on.

Partnership for Progress. "1927 Richard Wright." fedpartnership.gov/minority-banking-timeline/richard-wright.

Report, Tribune Staff. "Mae Reeves, 104, Pioneering Milliner." *The Philadelphia Tribune*, December 30, 2016. phillytrib.com/obituaries/mae-reeves-pioneering -milliner/article_64c15886-75f1-516b-9fa4-602967d9225e.html.

"Retired Milliner, 97, Honored by Smithsonian; Credits God for Success." *Catholic Standard*, November 1, 2010. cathstan.org/news/local/retired-milliner-97-honored -by-smithsonian-credits-god-for-success.

"Smithsonian Honors Philadelphia Hat Maker Mae Reeves." *Good Black News*, July 28, 2010. goodblacknews.org/2010/07/28/smithsonian-honors -philadelphia-hat -maker-mae-reeves.

Smithsonian. "Showstoppers: Mae Reeves of Philadelphia Vintage Hat Collection." YouTube, May 18, 2011. Video, 1:24:34. youtube.com/watch?v=Tlk2BoXXnjE&t=939s.

Taylor, Erica. "Little Known Black History Fact: Church Hats." *Black America Web*, February 19, 2013. blackamericaweb.com/2013/02/13/little-known -black-history-fact-church-hats/.

Thulin, Lila. "Entrepreneur Mae Reeves' Hat Shop Was a Philadelphia Institution. You Can Visit It at the Smithsonian." Smithsonianmag.com, June 26, 2019. smithsonianmag.com/smithsonian-institution/maes-millinery-shop-was-philadelphia-institution-and-polling-site-you-can-visit-it -smithsonian-180972475/.

Tmvp1productions. "Mae Reeves Interview.mov." YouTube, December 12, 2011. Video, 3:25. youtube.com/watch?v=sd79682qFoY.

Tmvp1productions. "Mae Reeves Live Interview." YouTube, December 23, 2014. Video, 1:58. youtube.com/watch?v=bZcCnRWn_jk.

Tmvp1productions. "Mae Reeves Millinery Shop.mov." YouTube, December 23, 2014. Video, 33:59. youtube.com/watch?v=XGvydyJ7HU8.

Wang, Hansi Lo. "Mae Reeves' Hats Hang at National Museum of African American History and Culture." NPR, September 18, 2016. npr.org/sections /codeswitch/2016/09/18/493758448/mae-reeves-hats-hang-at-national-museum-of-african-american-history-and-culture.